Take your journal everywhere you go along with your coloring book and pencils.

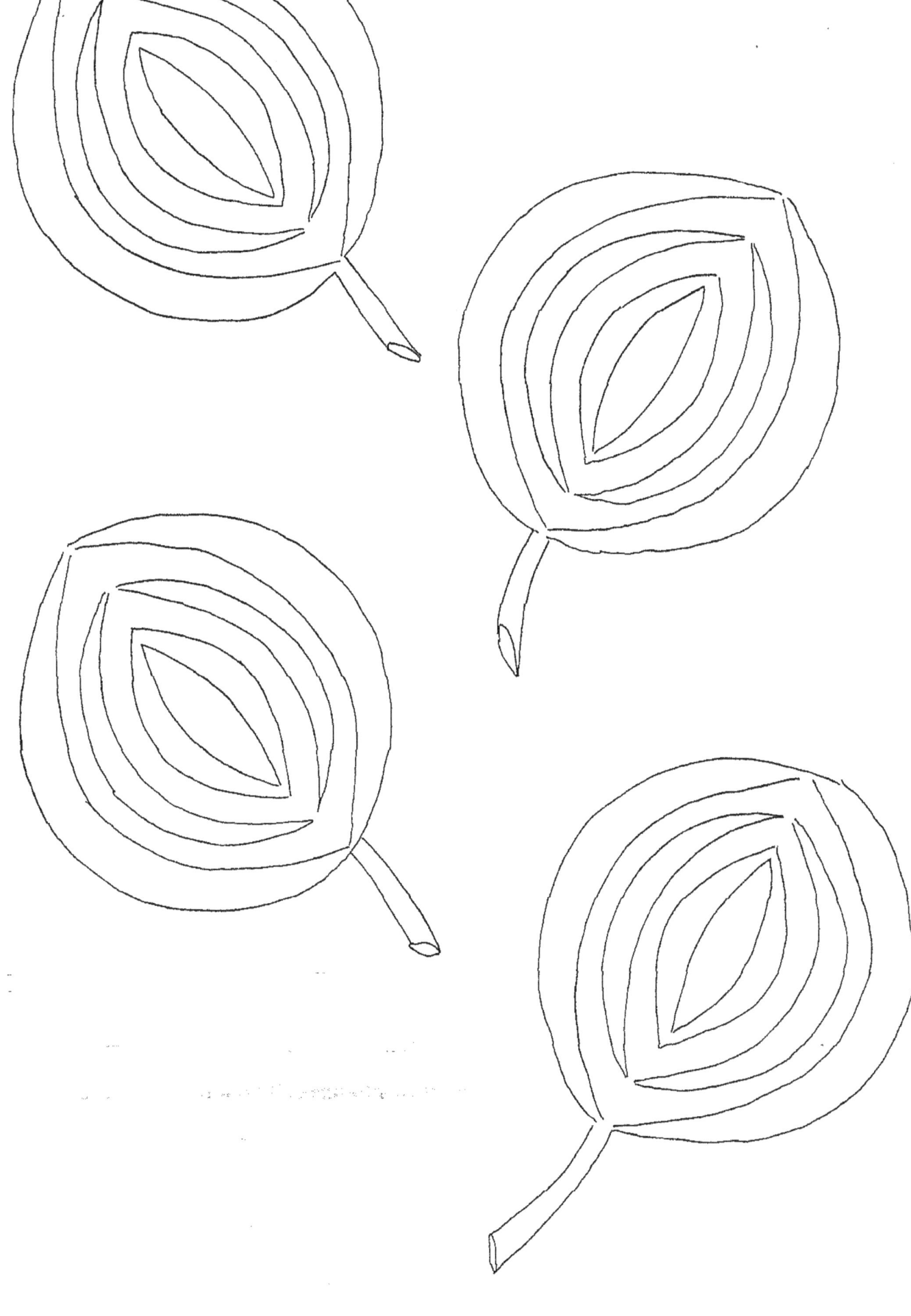

Write a story in your journal.

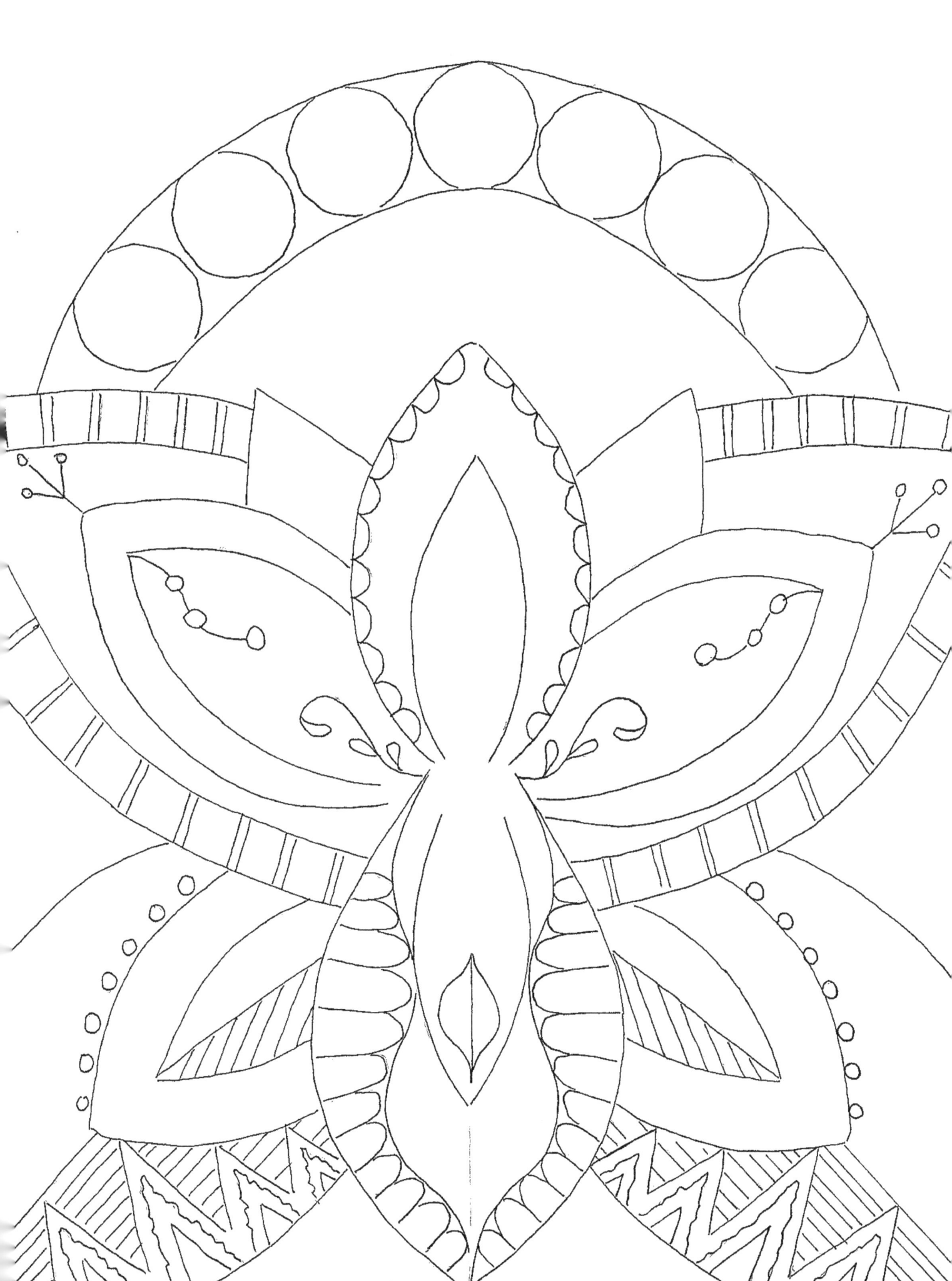

Write about things that help you make sense of your life in your journal.

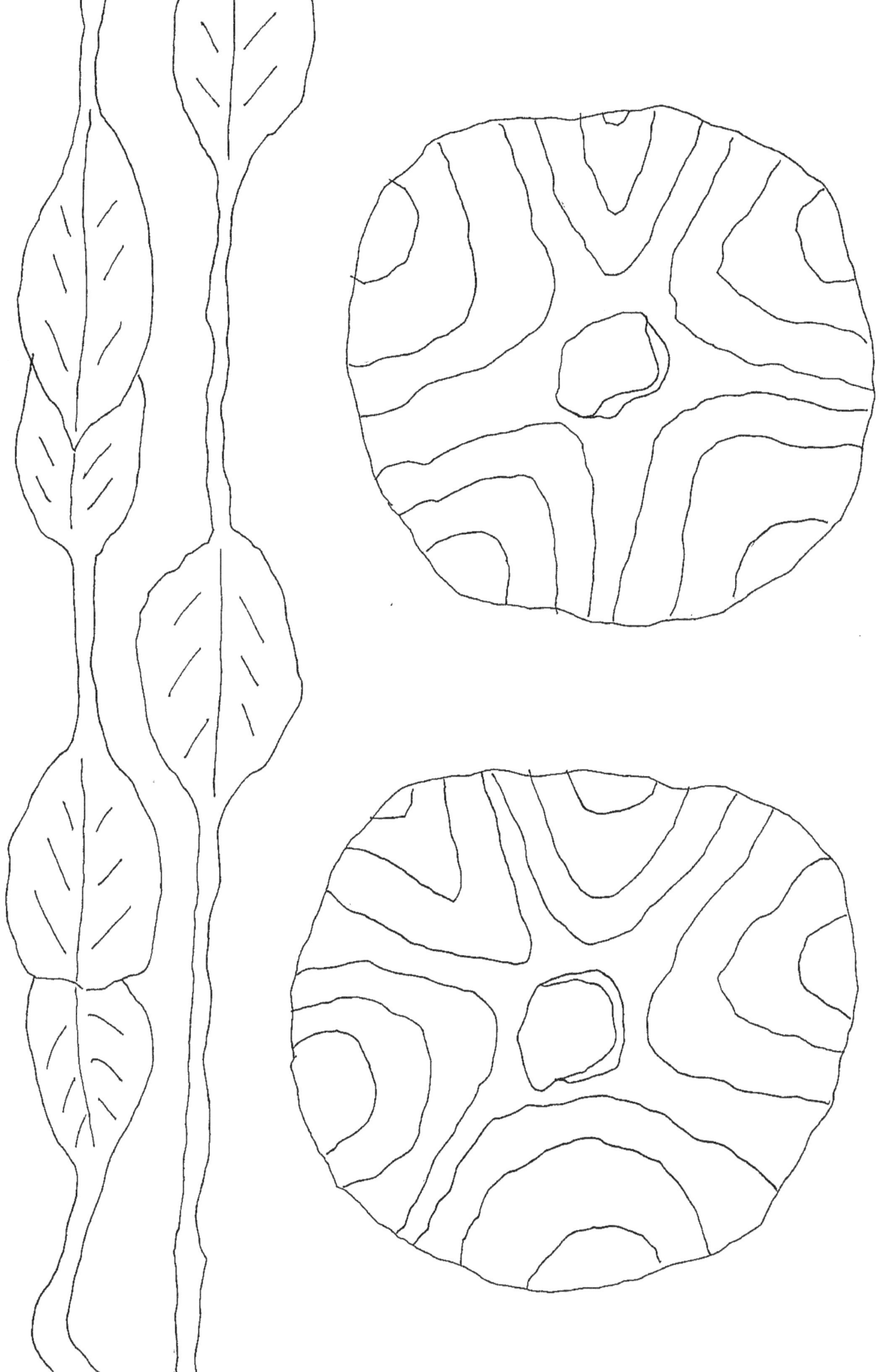

Keep a list of books you want to read in your journal.

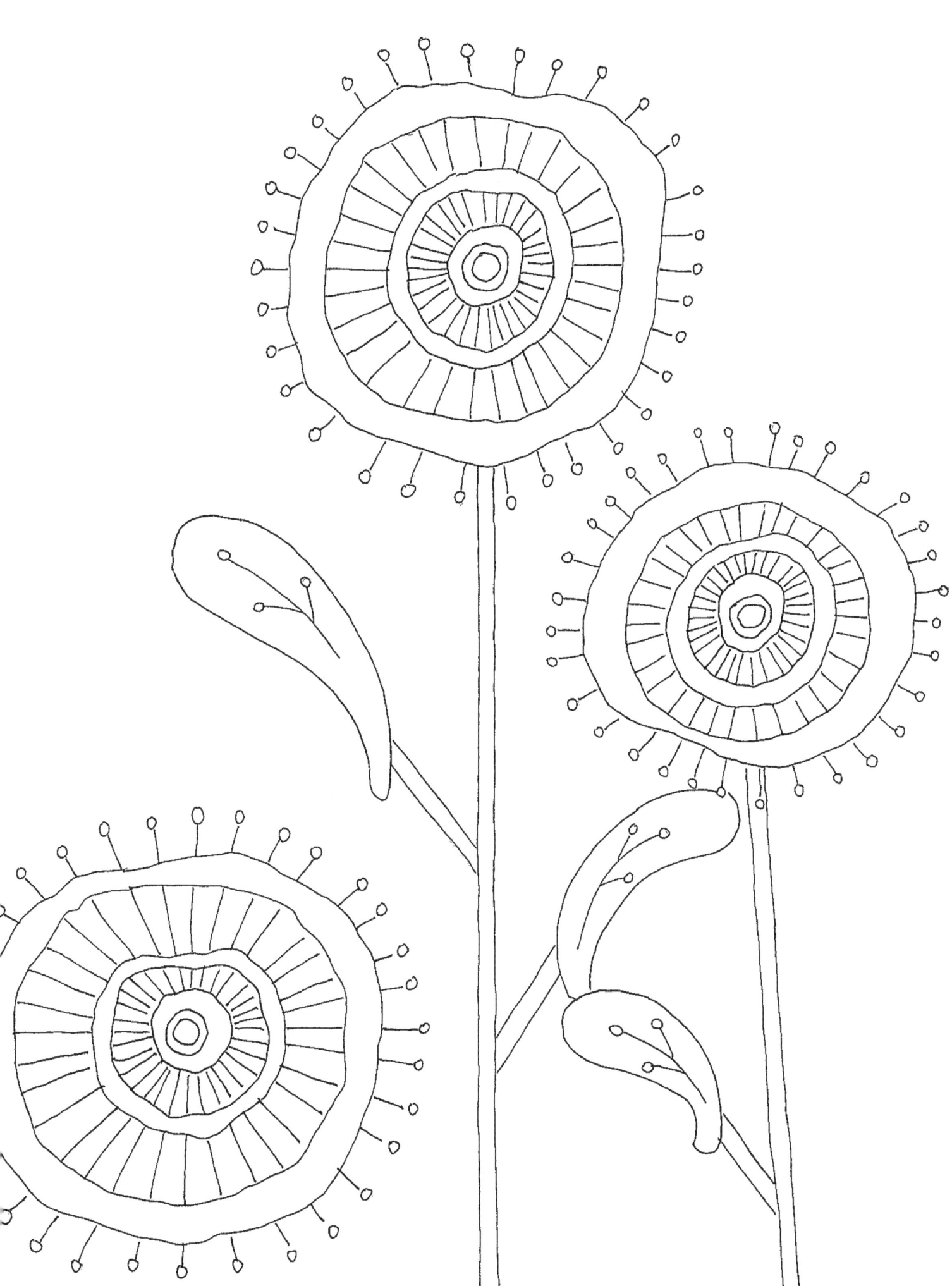

Writing in your journal accesses the left side of your brain, the analytical and rational side.

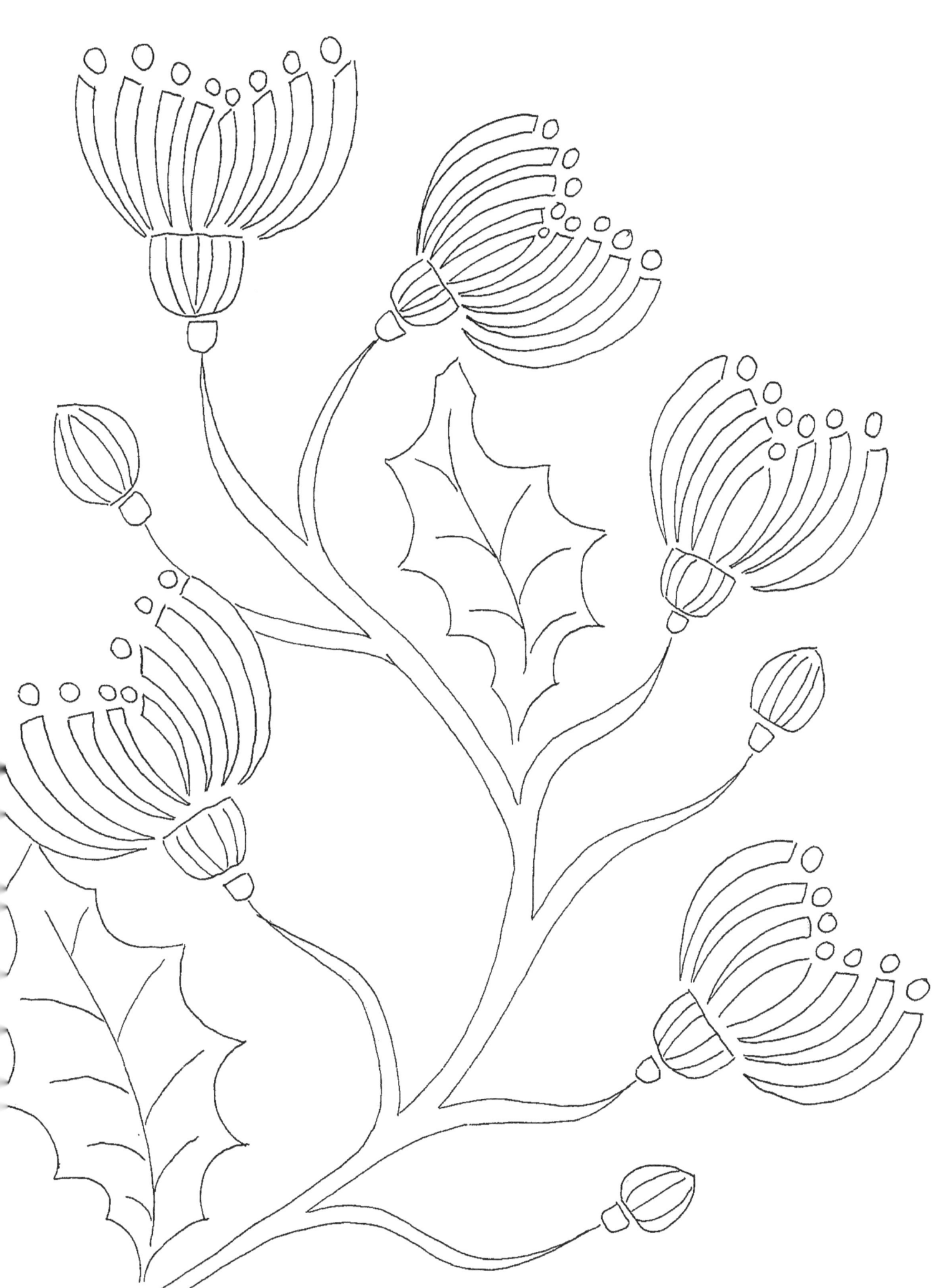

Write about all your successes in your journal.

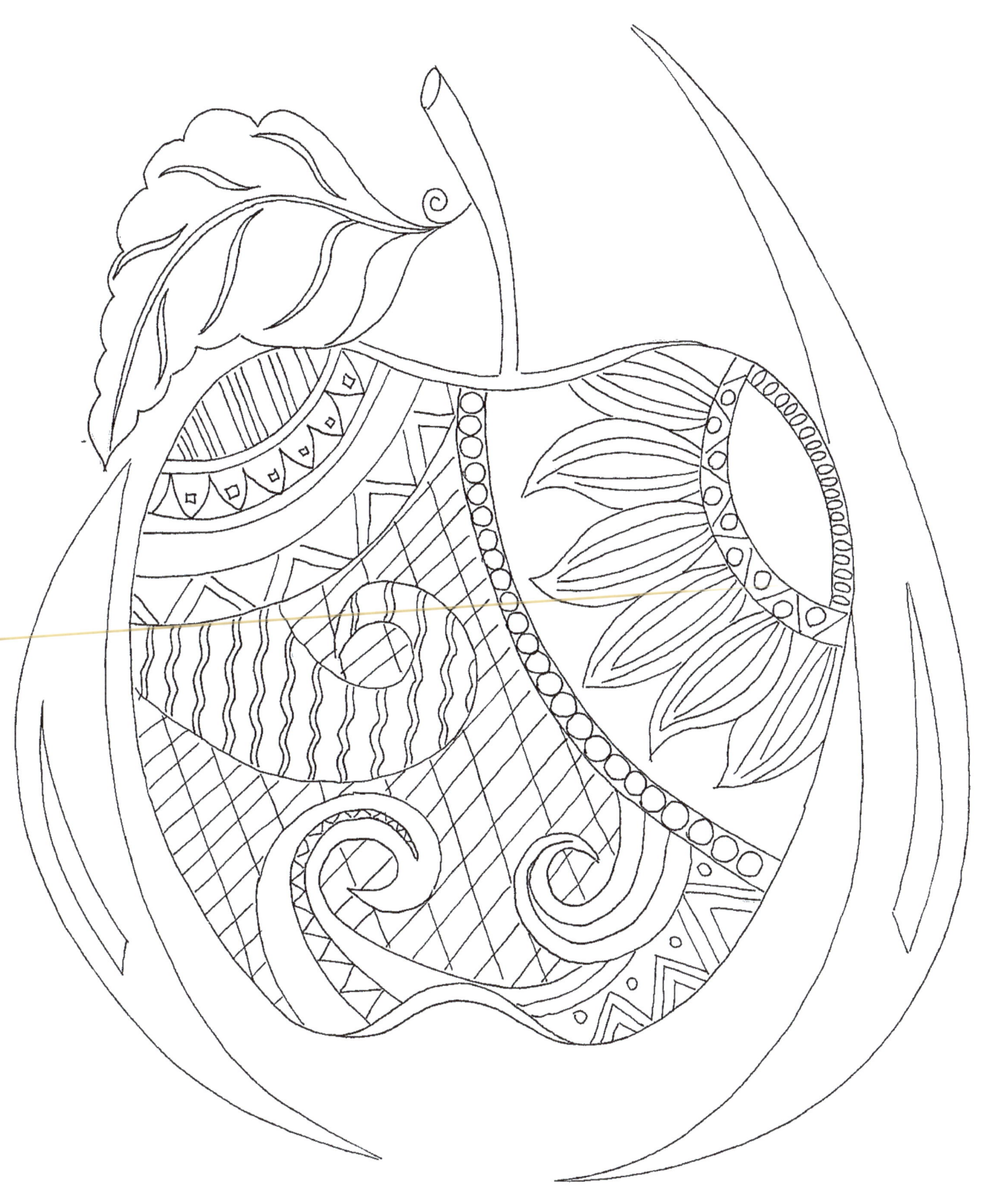

Record a journal of your favorite quotes.

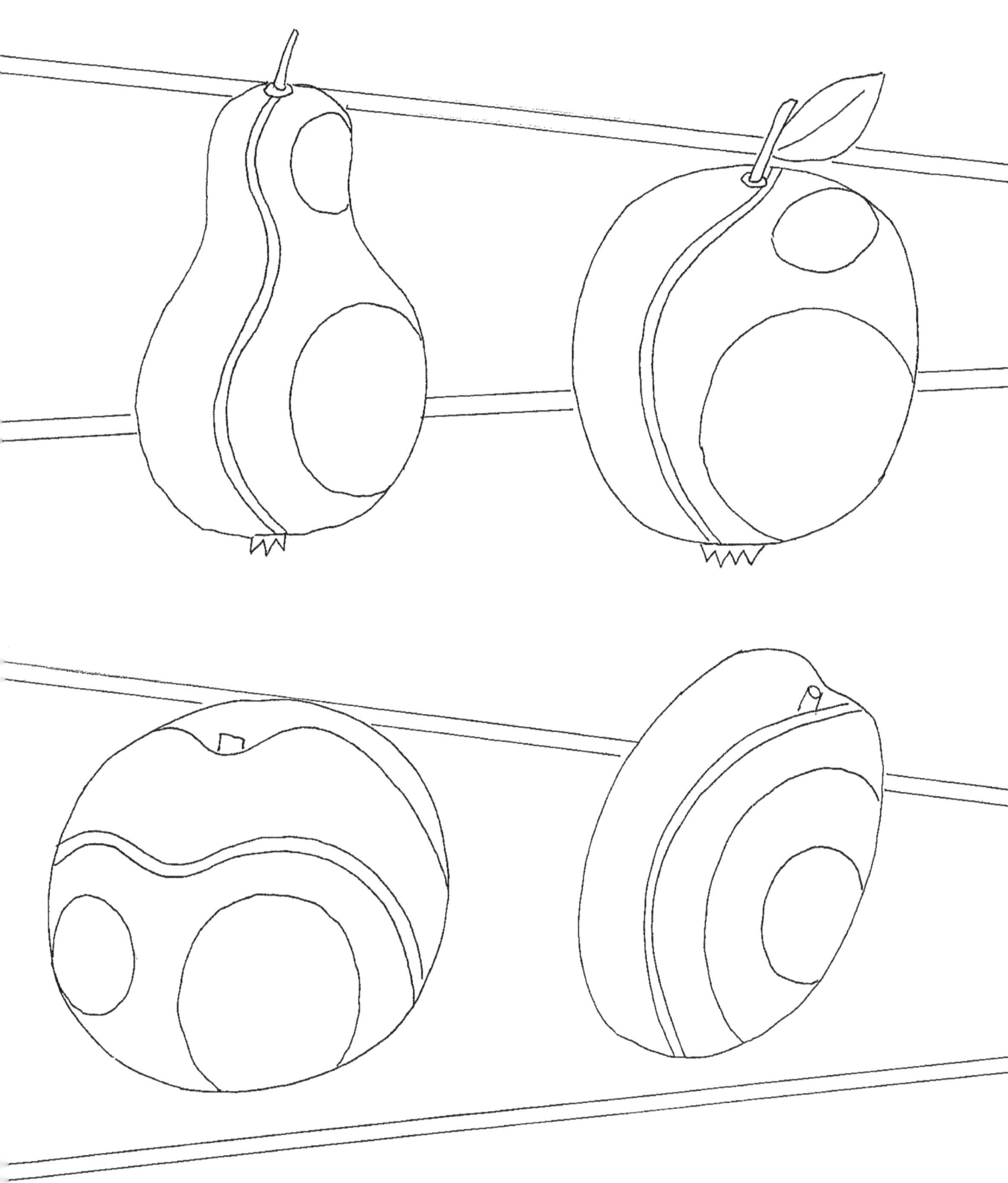

Develop your intuition by writing in a journal.

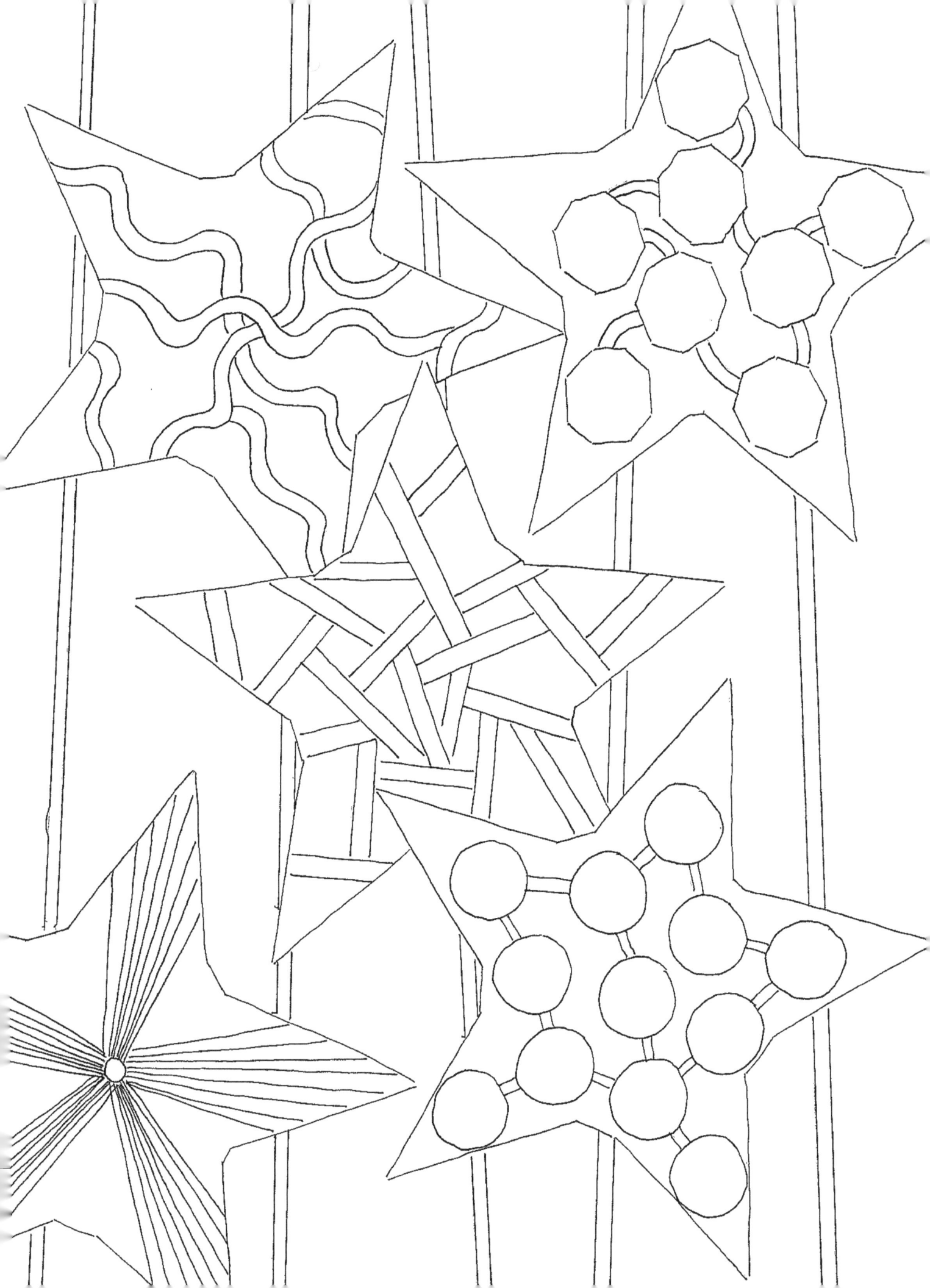

Keep a record of all your favorite songs.

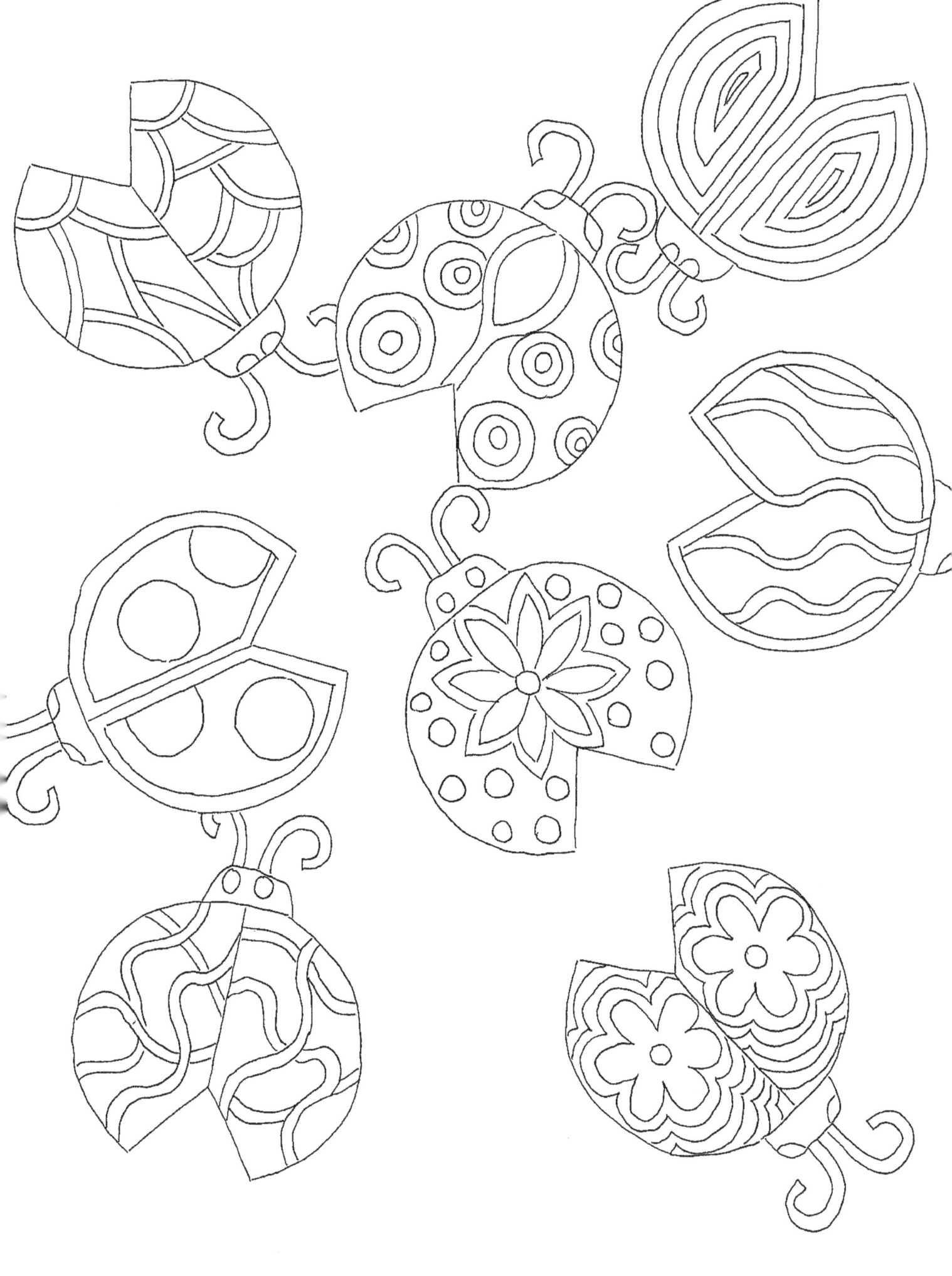

Keep a nature diary to connect with the natural world.

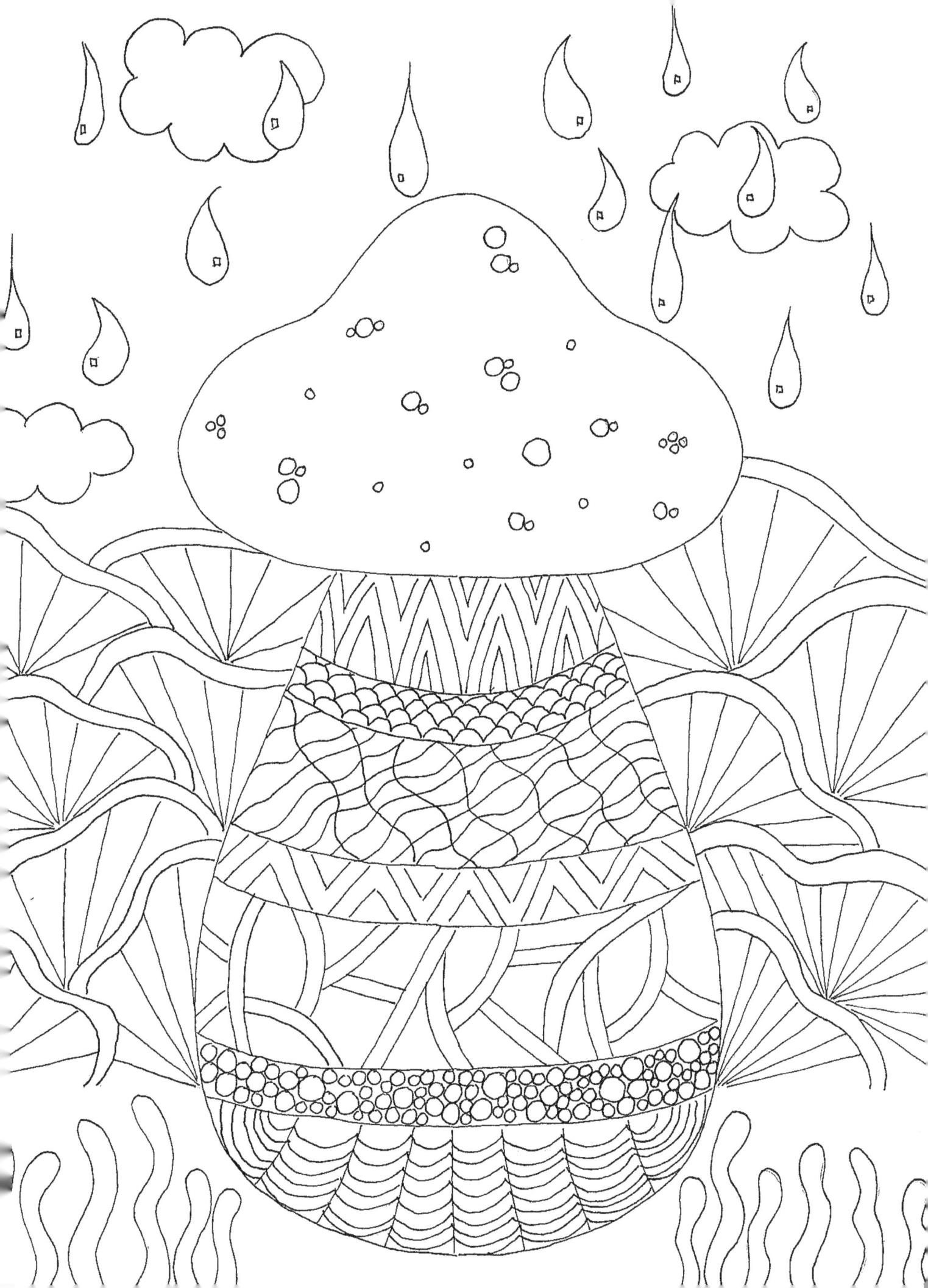

Writing in a journal will help you recover from grief and loss.

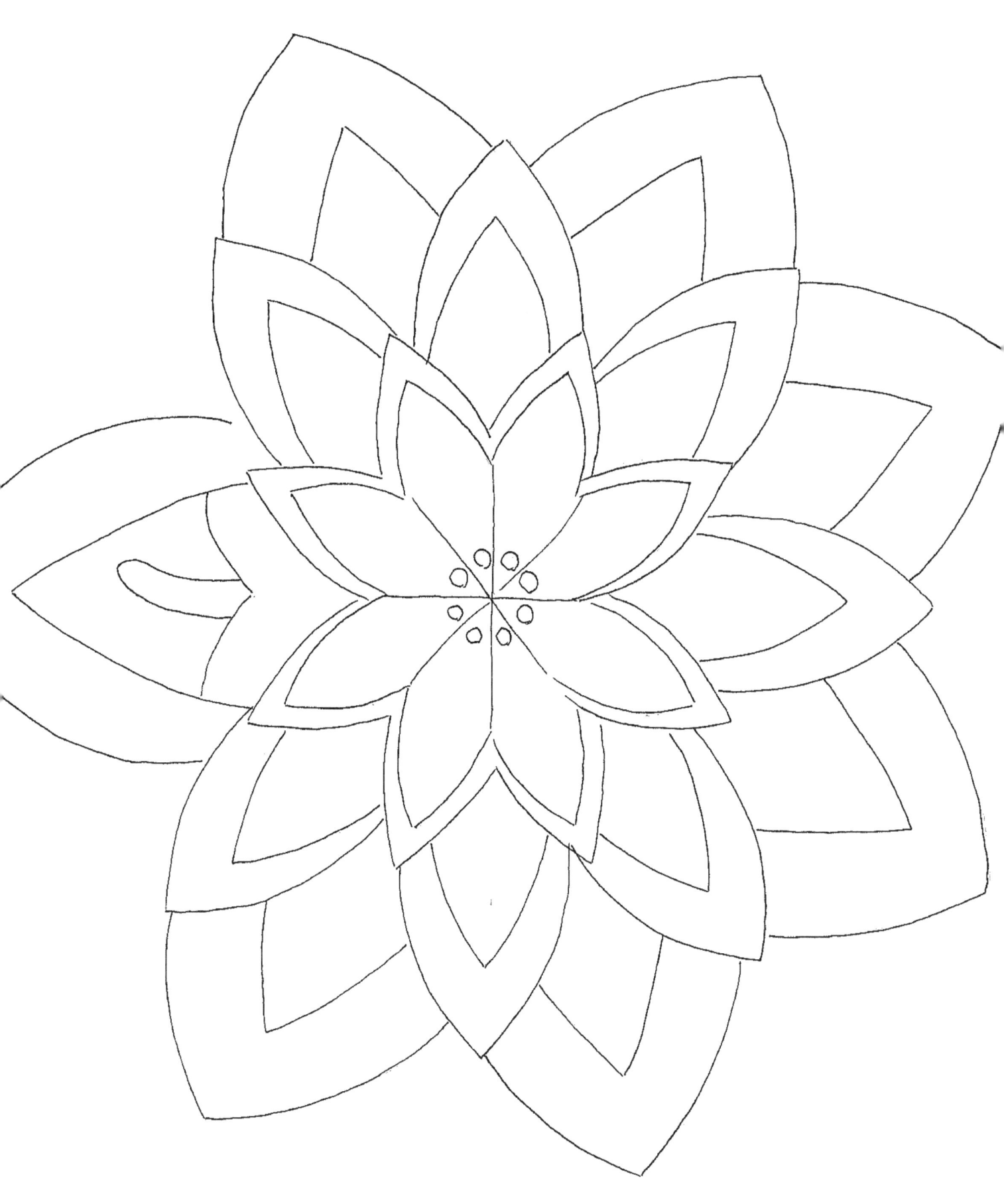

Start a journal of self-portraits or "selfies"

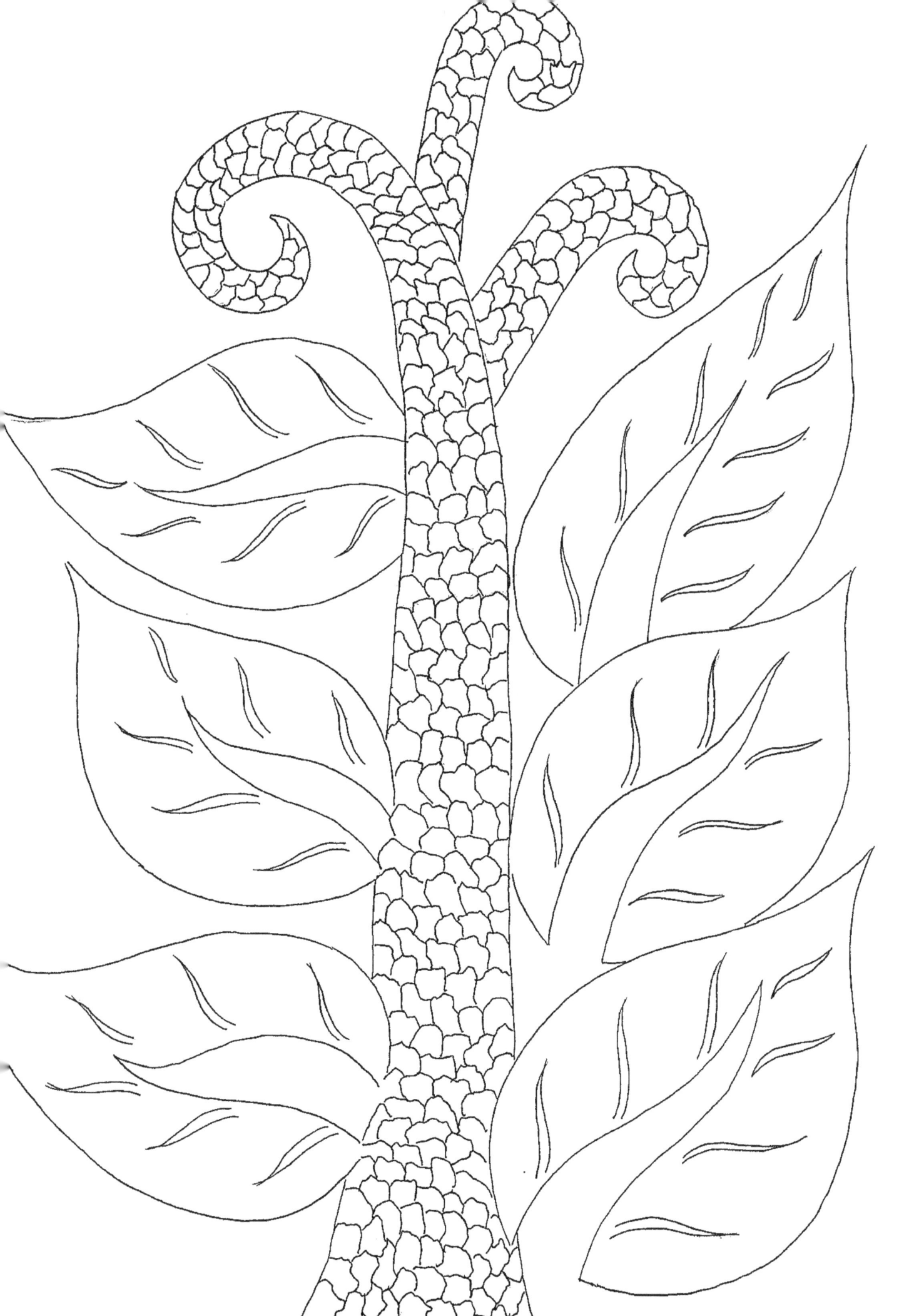

Improve your perspective on life and clarify issues by writing in a journal.

List things you would like for your children to know about you.

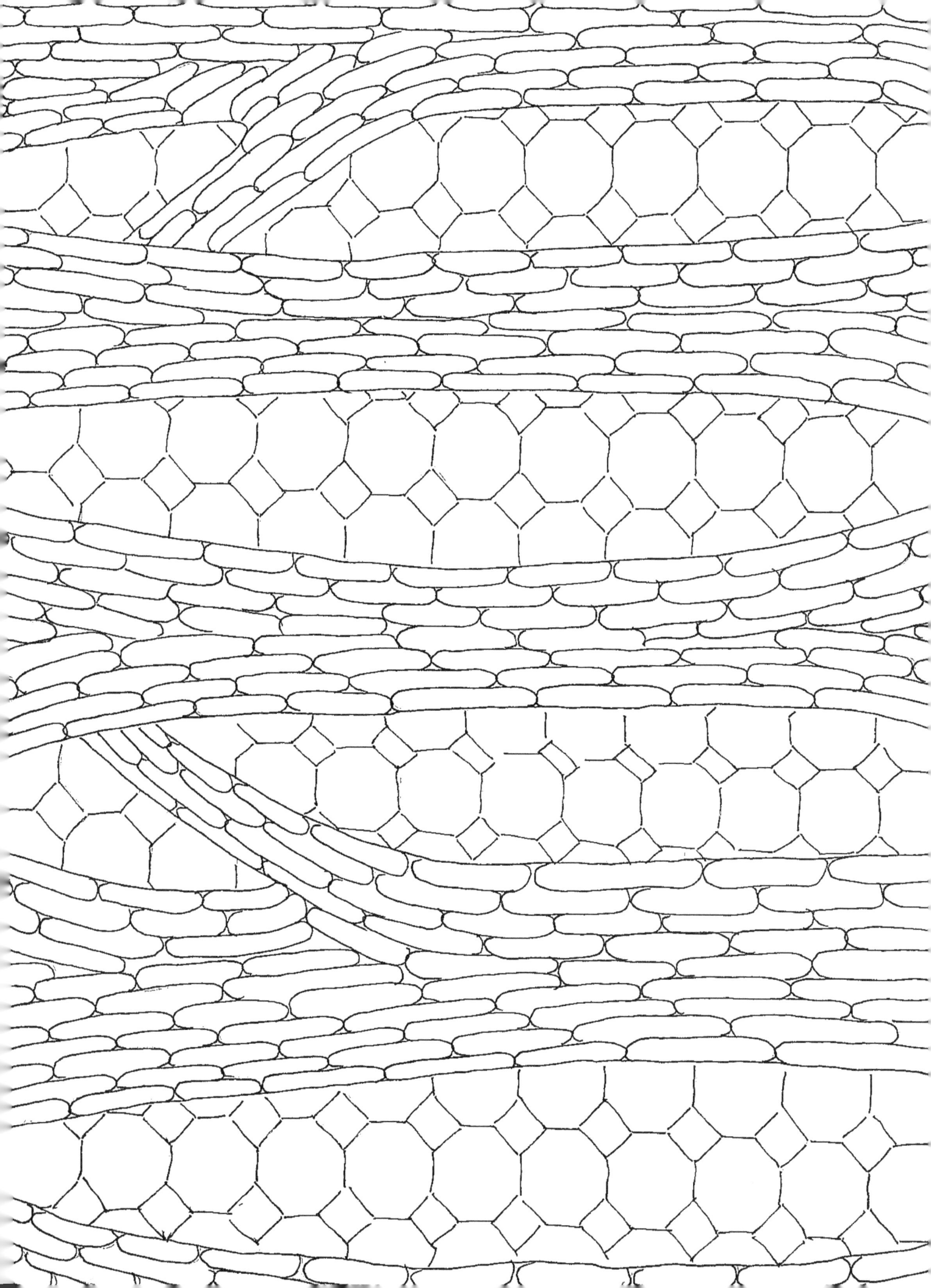

Make a journal list of childhood memories.

Write down skills and qualities you see in yourself.

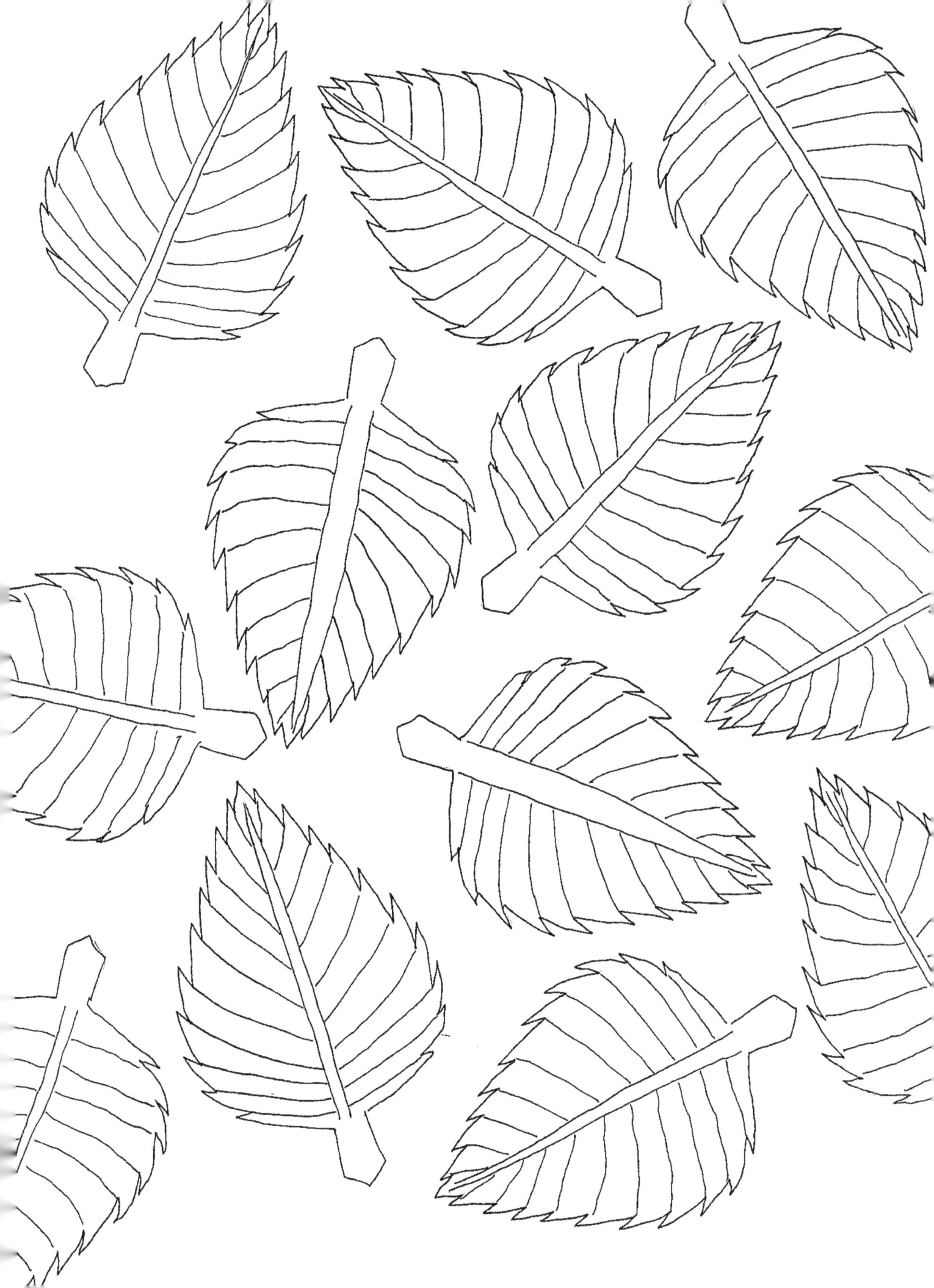

Make a list of things that you find hard to share.

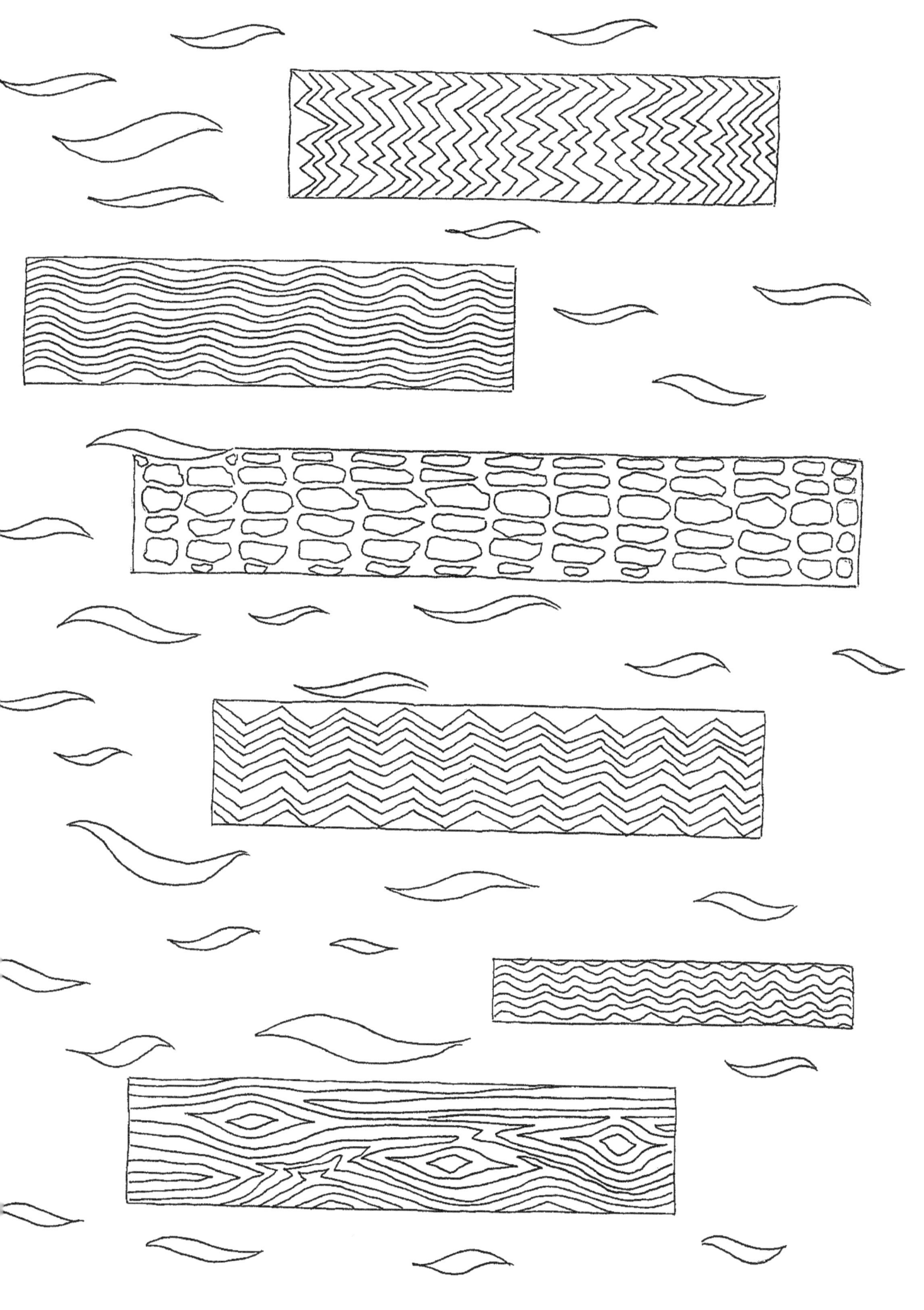

Journal ways you would like to make money.

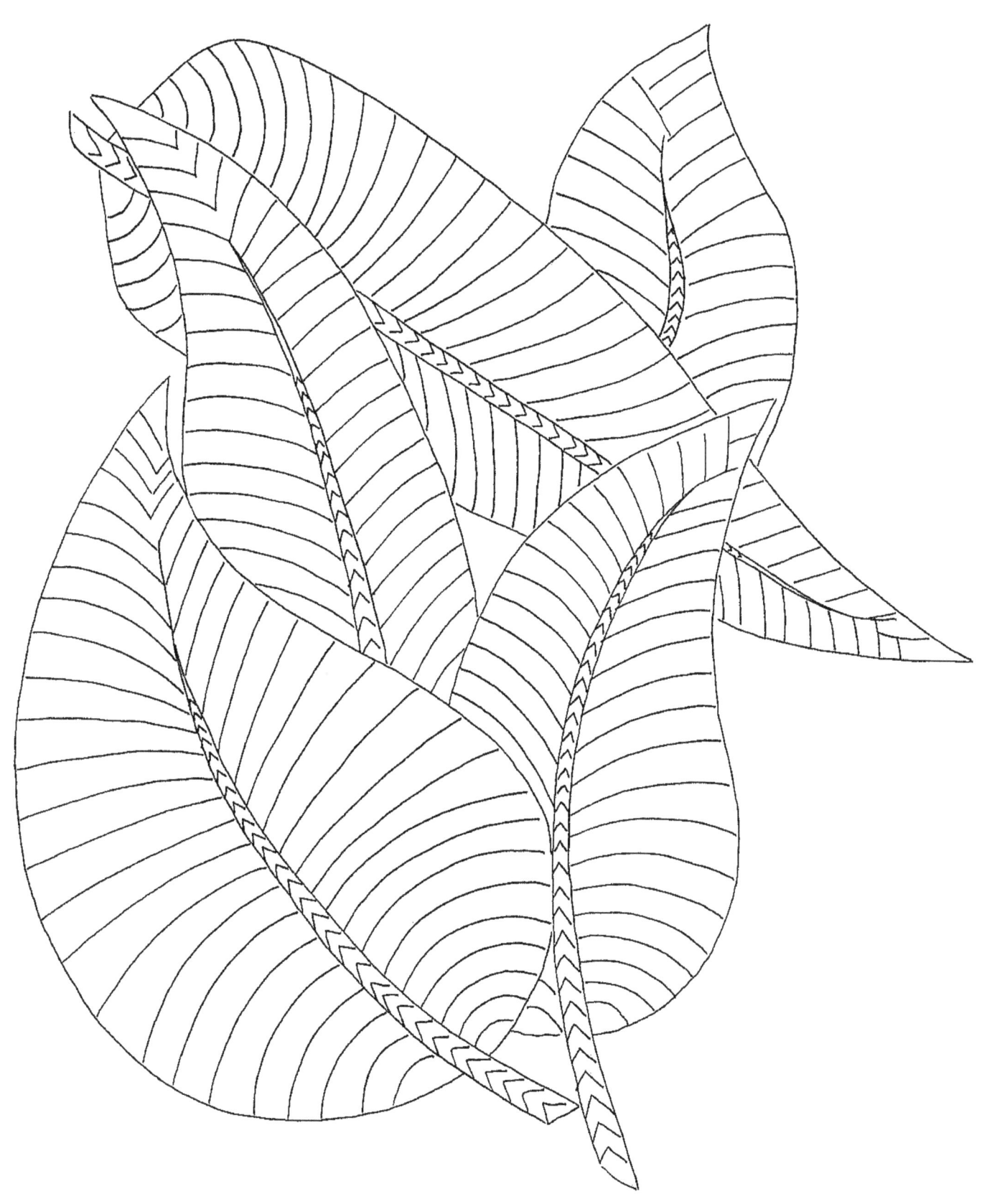

List ways you help others in your journal.

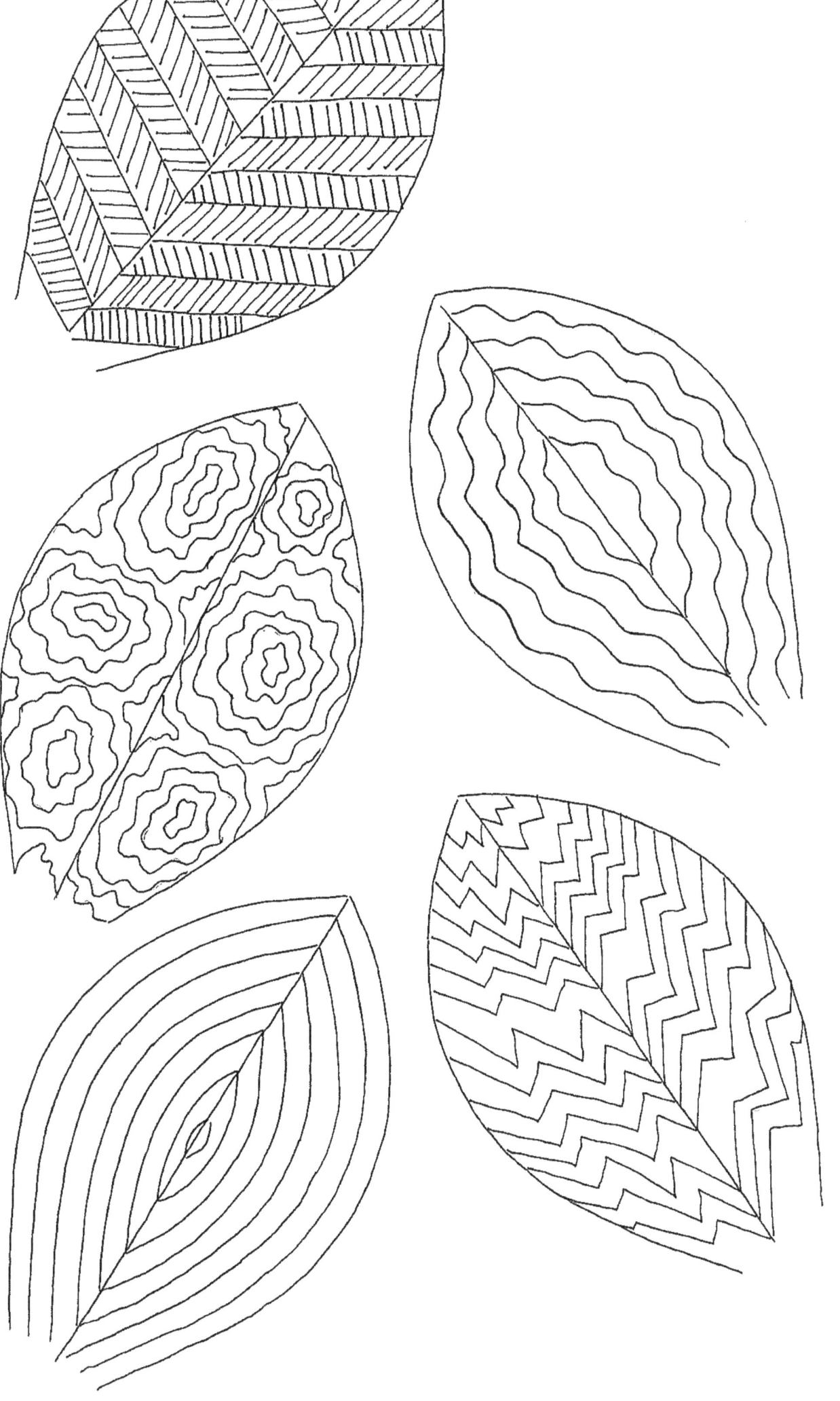

In your journal list some of the jobs you would like to have.